T0286914

ALSO BY DANIELLE VOGEL

Edges & Fray

The Way a Line Hallucinates Its Own Linearity

Between Grammars

A LIBRARY OF LIGHT

Danielle Vogel

WESLEYAN UNIVERSITY PRESS

A Library of Light

MIDDLETOWN, CONNECTICUT

Wesleyan University Press

Middletown CT 06459

www.wesleyan.edu/wespress

2024 © Danielle Vogel

All rights reserved

Manufactured in the United States of America

Designed by Crisis

Library of Congress Cataloging-in-Publication Data

Names: Vogel, Danielle, author.

Title: A library of light / Danielle Vogel.

Description: Middletown, CT: Wesleyan University Press, 2024. | Series: Wesleyan poetry |
Summary: "Combining incantation, elegy, documentary poetics, and lyric memoir,
this book is a raw recounting of the author's mother's tragic death entwined with a
book-length meditation on light, language, and lineage."—Provided by publisher.

Identifiers: LCCN 2023031619 (print) | LCCN 2023031620 (ebook) |
ISBN 9780819500915 (cloth) | ISBN 9780819500885 (ebook)

Subjects: LCGFT: Poetry.

Classification: LCC PS3622.O345 L53 2024 (print) |
LCC PS3622.O345 (ebook) | DDC 811/.6—dc23/eng/20230731

LC record available at https://lccn.loc.gov/2023031619

LC ebook record available at https://lccn.loc.gov/2023031620

5 4 3 2 1

for my motherline

I see the fissure in the subject (the very thing about which he can say nothing).

—Roland Barthes

I am telling you your own past, I want to explain it to you, I want to cure you of it.

—Violette Leduc

Build a house

with walls which come into existence

only with the particular prism effect

created by sunset

If necessary, some walls or parts of

the walls can be made of material other

than light

—Yoko Ono

CONTENTS

Light

,

We come to life now. When we. When we are. We pick up language like
a lit garment, wet and shaken out. A shinbone lifts. An elbow. A para-
graph. All shot through until our edges dissolve in pleats. We are held
together through our separatenesses. We are an ambiance of remains.
Wreckage, re-configuring. We are an illuminated architecture. Nothing
you know to name. We are a moving letter. Topologies of sound. We
are never static, but echoic. As we make shape, we take it. The mouth,
unmarooned. We trespass punctuation. A curvature. An arc, unarchived
in the sharing. We almost make a circle, but what we mean is silence
into sound. Or a coming into focus. We are always in the present tense.
The flood of the gap, washed out. We, a word. We, a window. Bring
your body.

,

*

When we are six, we are also seventeen. When we are six, we are
reading. But we cannot yet read. Our language drapes over some thing
and we make shape associatively. When we are seventeen, we are
reading by resonance. A certain rhyme in the curve of an atom. The
slight of it slips through the tongue. A leaning of throats. When we are
three, we are also fourteen. When we are fourteen, we do not know the
difference between a book and a body. We are unbound, gutterless.
A woman's skin near the eye. We are a page, the plum-colored aureole.
A cobbled finger-bone, a vague star system.

*

'

A slope of cells. Or water, stories. A soft warping through the gloss.
A belly. We refuse to come into convergence. We are already con-
verged. We are the yellow hour that laminates the horizon. We are a
strigosing of selves. We love. When we are. When we are there. When
we are one, we are sometimes also twelve. When we are three, the
ground is mostly ether. We walk through the specter of things. When
we are seven, the world is drained. When we are only four, we live in
empty hours. When we are six, we fall in love with the position of a sun,
the slats between astronomical bodies. We fall in love. We love through
the throat. We reverberate. We are wedded in occurrence. We are led
by our hands, but we have no hands. When we are nine, we are also
twenty. We are a shifting geometry, the rotation of a sound, and the
halo moves from the window.

'

'

When we are. When we are there, we lay together and cover ourselves with our voices. When we are ten, we are also twenty-one. We speak of breathing, but this is a thing we cannot do. When we are seven, we are also eighteen. When we are eighteen, we begin our bodies. But we are unmappable, unhinged. A resynchronization of codes, the crystalline frequencies of stars, seeds, vowels, lying dormant within you. We are the oldest dialect. A sound the voice cannot make but makes.

'

of Light

’

I don't know how I began but when I imagine it, I see a single illumi-
nated line. A light like electricity. A soft blue current. Breathing, vibra-
tory, becoming almost white, almost pink, as it ripples slowly in a total
darkness. Brighter now, a sound resonating, an intention recommitted
to. And as the line arches and turns, gathering incandescence, points
of light like voices, I know exactly what this light means to communi-
cate. Its meaning opens a door in my face, and I am contained, but
infinitely met.

’

All living creatures emit a radiance not visible to the human eye. The
brilliance of our glowing animal bodies fluctuates across the day.

Inside each of us, an unimaginable frequency. The coil-like contraction
of each strand of DNA vibrating several billion times per second, in
every cell. And with each contraction, one single biophoton—a light
particle—is released, generating this luminescence of the cells.

’

Our imperceptible glow, an intelligence. This source material. Cells communicating, lineage learning. Cells and stars composing, as they burn, as they write, a highly structured light field that nets all bodies.

*

This field is the first inscription. A crackling pulse that set me going. I think words like *amniotic*, *birth*, *origin*, *beginning*.

*

When the density of a star's core is created. When fused atoms contract to cause expansion. When the shape of me is interrupted by grief, by awe, by the regularity of a day. With all its intermittences. Its windows through time, reversing order.

*

When energy moves into matter, time begins. But in its elasticity, the light gets threaded.

*

My favorite memory of my mother is stored in a photograph I no longer have. She stands in a steel-blue oversized sweater and jeans in our backyard by the neighbor's fence. The cherry tree, before the lightning struck, behind her in bloom. The sun, as it sets, makes a halo of her hair. She glows, a corona, at the photograph's center. She's pregnant with my brother, but I don't think you can tell from the photograph; I know because I think I remember taking it.

'

The earliest memory of my body comes from outside of it. Long slats of a crib in shadow. A dim yellow light forming the hallway, gray and particled at its edges, outside my bedroom door. My mother's voice from another room. Before language, just sonorous music. And in the absence of her physicality, I feel my own voice for the first time, vibrating the shape of me.

'

I am comfortable in most kinds of darkness. Darkness allows nearness to the most intimate unknown. That place from which I first arrived. The door of me, my mother. What color was the inside of her body? What color was my consciousness there?

'

I am attempting to get through the door of me. Through the door of my mother's body and her mother's body before her and so on, straight into the mouth of the very first light emitted.

'

We are accustomed to thinking ourselves individual, but so many of us feel unstable: of fracture, disembodiment or conjoinment to something unnameable, some *thing* other than ourselves. A kind of microchimer-ism. A persistent presence of an *other* or *elsewhere*. We are taught to mistrust this intimacy.

'

Consider the human body. Mine and yours, composed mostly of water, of light. Consider the information stored within the nucleus of one zygote.

Within my body and yours, a coherent, ancestral light.

'

Between a mother and her fetus, the placenta, an organ relating and connecting forms. A conduit for exchange, for migrating cells. And those cells may take up residence in the body of the other. Integrating the tissue.

'

And somewhere, on the other side of time, is everything.

'

Sometimes, when asked what I'm working on, I tell people I'm writing a translation of light. Light, like the memory of a color, of a sound that we can't quite sense, but is there, nonetheless. Inherited light. Cellular light. Interstellar. Memories that have already happened to someone or some- where else.

'

As a child, I felt a grief in me that was too large to be only my own. By three years old, I realized I could absorb the sensations of others. It was a feeling of light, of concave patterns of energy moving from others and into me. I would stand close to my mother and absorb her anger, her loneliness, her worry, and I would replace it with a calmer light.

'

The world through which I moved seemed an apparition. I lived slightly off-center in that hologram. I moved through the echo, guided by some invisible magnetism. Some edgeless halo, some throat of light. The world humming, without certain form. Everything and everyone seemed to glow, to emit an atmosphere.

I listened for the dialectics of this internal light. I learned to read a writing with no certain alphabet. A language that accessed and organized the body's unseen energy fields.

*

To start, now, at myself, this ledge of a blue line, this pigment glossed into a buff. A cloud. A stroke of color approaching shadow. To begin again crouched inside the word *birth*. A body. Before form, the sonority of her.

*

To correct the imbalances within. To start at the most unseen.

*

For a long time, I felt as if I, the very essence of my *self*, was something akin to an atmosphere caught inside of a body that was not my own. My physical form was unfamiliar, slightly frightening. I had great guilt over inhabiting it. I was a kind of spectral dislocation I came to love.

I found gifts there, in this dislocation. Ways of sensing what was invisible. I tried to meet those invisible places with my own. Eventually placing words in the expanse, and watching as, through grammar, they contracted, shedding light. *Meaning, sound, relation.*

'

Light lets the grid of a thing respire. Each intersection becomes an *or* in relation. Imagine the skin of you, all its points of convergence, either through sense or sound, being met at once. The grid begins to glow.

We move in every direction even standing still. We are let by light. It culls something against us. The grid is refracting. Light oracles us. Languages us. Reflexes relation. I become beside myself and something else even while stationary.

'

As language contracts, I experience my form. Its skin, sensors and bones, its joints and synapses. Language is erotic, sensory. Atmospheric and physical. The living bridge between the two.

'

Language, like light, is an immaterial medium through which all things energy and matter move. And like light, language causes micro-distortions within us.

I hold language close and with much reverence. And what is most astonishing to me is that *this* is a body—a lingual-body—I might share with others.

I compose a sentence and put it on with another. I speak it into the space between us. I place it directly into a mouth through having written it for reading. I wear it with another. Walk down its center and in all directions, thinking in tandem with someone else. We make corresponding shapes and then we move apart having exchanged something irrevocable.

,

The energy structure of a star, of language, of my mother. When the atomic forces that support our structures are exactly equal to the gravitational forces which collapse us. When we move toward our own dense centers. When we collapse while expanding outward. The core of a mother. All the heavy elements that compose her.

,

For many years, I tried to find my body. I kept language close.

*

As my mother's living body decayed, so did the house. Mold grew out of a flooded basement. The walls foxed with it. The bathtubs overflowed with clothes and garbage. Every drawer, closet, corner, and cubby in the house was littered with mouse feces. She smashed all the mirrors and swept the shards into my childhood bedroom. She stored empty vodka bottles beneath the couches. While cleaning the house after her death, I found a packet of cocaine stuffed into my brother's long-outgrown baby shoe.

*

I unwrap a word. A book and body. Always both. Inhabited and inhab-itable. Light like a skin, like a sound, shed. Shuttered. Shivered off. Hatched. Transformed. A page: a hallway of light between us. I want the body and book in all its tenses. Inhabited, inhabitable, inhabitation, inhabitability.

*

Those distances of electricity, outside of matter, within it, are enduring.

'

She deteriorated quickly without me in the house. There was an anger and loneliness I kept at bay with my presence but staying as long as I did nearly extinguished me. If I could do it again—But I do not want to inherit an early death. I write this book in the wake. She is not here so that I can be.

'

And sometimes I'd go days without being able to feel my body at all. To hold on to something. Any anchor. When the colors slur, slipping. Lucid and transparent, fading.

'

In the womb, fetal cells migrate into a mother's body altering her immune system often aiding in repair. And as this happens, a mother's cells pass learned information into her child's cellular makeup. It is in this way that transgenerational traumas can be hemmed into the body of a child who hasn't yet experienced the world.

′

When I was eleven, my mother bought me my first pair of eyeglasses.
To see the trees at the edge of the parking lot, the sharp tracery of
each leaf, even its smallest branches. To experience the distance of the
sky. To see my own feet on the pavement was dizzying. *I didn't know*, I
said. To go home and to see my own hand while reading. The book held
at such a distance that I wasn't completely eclipsed. To have learned
language in this way. Allowing for the borderlessness of all things. The
whole world breathing. With the soft matter between matter visible.
The whole room of the world blurry, full of gray, shivering particles.
To see my mother's form, unwavering, for the first time in my life.

′

When all limits are illegible. What is a body?

′

My mother spent many years living almost alone. The death of a
mother never becomes lost. It never dulls and incorporates itself into
the day. It only drones on, humming its tenor. Numbing other timbres
in its wake.

Look at what you see and light will leave its trace. In the retina. Against the immaterial of a body. Sight, at all levels of focus, never fails. It emits an invisible line that looms desire to disappearance to desire. Light, its originary source, never leaves you. I want to believe that language can preserve where I've been, but also that it can look at a thing and alter its reflection.

′

Sometimes I have a feeling of amnesia, as if I should, but can't— although it is almost reachable—remember from where I originated. And this feels like a color, exploded, a certain resonance I recognize between myself and this world that houses us.

′

A sentence to access a kind of hypnogogic gloss. To recall what I didn't know I could remember. To alter time and the body's light.

′

This earliest astral light, sidereal darkness, the conduit for all form, all thought. The childhood body of my mother standing on the steps of her

Brooklyn apartment. The childhood body of her mother, her mother's mother before her, coming into a harbor. Light, transferred to thought, is navigable. Time's mutability. Behind the corporeal.

*

Grief or love, light's dilation. The time of a body and the memory of that body in movement.

*

When I was small and still living with her, I wanted to write to all the dead people I had never met. I wanted to talk to those concentrations of energy I felt in the hallways of my house, my school's stairwell, the damp corners of my yard. What I wanted to say couldn't be arranged so I'd stay very still and reach my silence outward like a tactile glow, a static reaching to communicate with passing frequencies.

*

Tonight, I'd like to write to a dead woman at the bottom of this ocean in that same way. Sending out a kind of undercurrent that scripts itself into her, into me.

*

Writing isn't the same as looking. It isn't the same as touch, yet it embeds itself like something felt. A voice away from its body isn't irrelevant.

,

A residual vibration, some desire left behind in the wake of a physical departure. Grief is a ghost. Light is a ghost. Language. I've not been haunted by my mother but sometimes I hear an urgent crackle in the corner of the room that holds me.

,

Ash and sedimentation, silted up, slick and gummy slowly becoming fossil, memory. We sent her ash three hundred feet below sea level. A nautical urn to hold her. We gave her over to the inlet of the ocean. Handwritten letters on a nearly transparent paper, dissolving. The house is left behind. Her resonance in my DNA, my sight. I measure absence past, absence future.

,

Sometimes I experience my own edgelessness reaching out toward my mother's. Into skin, dust, cells, and desire. Now, she's been depleted to ash, dispersed. But what of that radiation. Can it be taken, intercepted, swallowed, rerouted?

*

Those who love me tell me I did the right thing. The only thing to be done. That I couldn't have done anything for her, but a part of me knows they're wrong. I was terrified. Of what she might do to me. It's true, she had become violent. But it wasn't only that. I was afraid of what being in her presence would erase in me. There's a kind of atmosphere in my body that I can only describe as "elsewhere." It's why I write, it's from where I love, it's from where I empathize, heal, teach. But in that elsewhere, there is also something that obliterates language and a cohesive identity. I love this place in me. I've learned to take care of it so that I can stay here for myself and others. It's a depth that I've inherited. I used to be afraid of it. I thought I needed to be alone to keep it manageable, but I've learned that this isn't true. Would I have been able to learn this if I were still caring for my mother, calibrating her moods to my own?

*

A componium of hauntings: my mouth, a barrel in conversation with the barrel of whatever housed me. With whatever was once there. With whatever slid up beside me taking my own solidity from me.

*

A book and a body exchange walls, thresholds. To write to a dead woman. To cross the space in the house where she died—sitting in a desk chair rolled into the kitchen—cradling a folded bed pillow against her womb. To cross the equator of this sentence.

,

Seeing her in her coffin, laid out at the mouth of the funereal room, I hadn't seen her for over six years, but the night before, I washed for her: a pair of jeans, black underwear, socks, a black sleeveless silk shirt. I folded her favorite gray blazer, bleach-flecked black Converse. I bought her a bra; I couldn't find any that weren't covered in mold. I gathered her earrings, and her favorite necklace that looked like and was as large as a man's dress tie fashioned of glass crystals. None of this would be seen. I brought these things to another house that is a funeral home. Two days later, all of it would be burned with her body, but her house would still stand, even though two weeks before she had set fire to its kitchen.

,

The focal point of a body. Of a house. Of a book. Currents of light and sound. Alignment and introspection burned out. All the imperceptible inner forces. One's highly charged inner expanse, replete with harmonies.

*

I kept her ashes in my home for a year before I took them to the ocean. Ash is a symbol of grief or repentance. The powdery remains of fire. To burn. To glow. To dry up, to parch. Our boat, above three hundred feet of salt water; her urn sank too quickly. What will the water give her? That new state of her body. *Penitence* comes from the Old French *paene* meaning *nearby, almost*. Meaning *is not enough*. To feel such regret for one's worth. One's living. I would have carried her ashes around with me everywhere had I been able to do it in secret. What I mean is that someone—quite a few someones—love me. So, I keep my sanity close for them.

*

I can't tell if writing incorporates what feels disassociated or furthers the distance between objects, but I come to language no matter. Language leaves its trace, as does silence, as does light. An induction of the cells.

*

The complexity of the present tense. We all have to do the work of living. And I want to live for myself and others through my work.

’

When light no longer has a medium: her body. If the frequency were to be infinitely dispersed.

’

After my mother's body was removed from the house, a survey began. I don't know how to directly write about grief or decay, but I'm trying. I make sentences, but the effects remain far off, beyond the margins, in the drifts and gutters of me. I want to heal her. I hadn't seen her for years, but I wanted to protect her still. I wouldn't let anyone empty her drawers or closets, but I wanted nothing to do with the attic and basement. The whole house was coated in a filth unlike anything I'd ever seen. A living filth. A fungus and stickiness all over everything. The cups in the cabinets had layers of lipstick along the rim. The ashtray held three different brands of cigarettes and all of her packs were filled with collected butts. But what astonished me more than the filth was that despite it all, she still kept journals. She still read. There were hardcover books stacked in every room. She had been living and, in that time, had taken up habits like collecting rocks from the beach down the block. There were bowls of them on the kitchen table. Each about the size and heft of a hand.

*

A long time ago, I learned that when a mouse gives birth to a sick baby, it might eat it, taking it back into its body. I want to know how close the womb is to the stomach. The heart to the moon. I wanted to eat the entire house, its filth and stones, its feces, its mold, its shards of everything. I tell the moon I'd like to be like it. Reflective, gravitational, complete in all its phases, regardless of illumination. As I stand looking at the moon, I let my feet pulse. I can no longer tell where the road begins or where the edge of my face is in relation to the night.

*

Both sound and light are wave phenomena, oscillating like the disturbed surface of water. If at the speed of light, time stops. If the speed of light is invariable and absolute. If both space and time are flexible, relative. What is the speed of light in memory, in the cells, in pigment inherited, event inherited but not lived in space as we understand it through the body's solidity.

What is the speed of light in language? This impossible question is what guides me.

*

To articulate, to find access to that amnesia, that light source that set my matter vibrating.

'

A poem: this inner geography of light, composed, breaking.

'

A syntax invented itself inside of me. As volcanoes do. As algae and lichen do. As suns and planets and solar systems do. As babies do.

The light of our cells: a filmy incandescence, as color and light pulse in ambulation.

You look to focus on the page, but language—as it enters and exits you—balances at the edge of dissolution.

'

An amnesia like an after-image stored in the cells. The blur of a fluctuant memory, a nearly ungraspable, residual light. Intensely vibrating planes of color. And through writing, I reach into that phenomenal space.

'

The fractal dimensions of language don't reverse time but remind us of time's nonlinearity. Time's orbit, like language's, rivers.

'

Between dissolution and coalescence. Merging and formlessness, meeting. Language focuses while unfocusing: draws our gaze inward and outward at once. The event of reading: a scattering impulse that happens within the gesture.

'

Consider parallel light rays (thought) falling on a converging lens (this sentence). When reading, your thinking touches mine, and, while doing so, your incoming ray of thought, as it enters the book, is refracted and kinked toward mine. Together, we compose a prism. Our thinking striates, scatters. To converge while diverging.

Each word I place in your mouth is a shutter. Opening a small interval of time to allow light to travel.

A trough of light. A crest of light. The velocity of light depends on the medium through which it travels.

I can't remember the first time light happened to me.

*

I want to know if writing can raise the dead in me. The act of lifting: myself, a memory, a mother. To rear. To make higher. To restore to life. A voice. The physical sense of. Children, to bring up. But I won't have children. I think of the phrase: *I was raised in*. I was raised means *brought up there*. Brought into being. Bring me up. From sleep, from bed. From one's body. To get to one's feet. From one's grief. Get up from the table. Be fit. Be proper. To travel. To journey. To rise from the dead. To originate (from). Occur, happen, come to pass; take place. I write a piece of rising ground. To get a rise out of (someone). My mother has. Taken place. Has. Come to pass.

*

Grief has a long passage. For months I referred to my mother's death in the present tense. My mother dies. Was what I said and wrote. What was this slippage? When I found out, I paced the floor until my knees left me. And then I crawled toward the bathroom, picked up an old toothbrush and proceeded to clean the room with it. I began under the claw foot tub. Stretched out, on my belly, my cheek pressed to the floor, I reached for the furthest corner.

*

I've always wanted to speak to the dead, but, I think now, I understand that I want to levitate the dead in me. To speak to some body inside my body that I haven't yet met. What is levitation? Where is it? The place of lightness. An event of buoyancy. To raise (a person) into the air. See *gravity*. See *grave*.

'

The suffix *–ion* appears in words to form nouns of state, condition, or action from verbs. Levitation. Creation. Cremation. See *carbon*. See *essence*. The etymologies of many words contain their opposites. From *cremate*, I arrive at *come to be*. What becomes, happened.

'

My whole life, up until the moment of her dying, I felt I was practicing my mother's death. I imagined all the ways she might die until she died. And then I recognized that her living was everywhere. *My mother dies.* Always only in the process.

'

I first learned about death by learning about heaven. Heaven seemed like a place I wanted to be. I couldn't understand why we waited. I didn't want to be on earth without my mother and father so why couldn't we just all die together and get there sooner. I knew about sin, but not about suicide.

'

Even though my mother terrified me sometimes. *Dies* instead of *died*. I can't get to the past tense of grief. Or absence. This act of naming. Of bringing a thing close by putting sounds through an action, an event, her person. My mother's name was Mary Terese. She didn't like for me to call her *mother* or *ma*. Just *mom*, sometimes *mommy*. But I can't remember saying those words to her anymore. My mother was born on May 2, 1955. I don't know the exact date of her death. I felt it before I knew. She was found on August 22, 2012, but the coroner said she might have died two days before that. I want to know why, as adults, we're expected to not grieve publicly. Grief is a private concern. I go to books to grieve. I go in the bathroom and close the door. I cry silently after my lover turns off the light in our bedroom at night, even though she'd prefer that I cried out in the open. As a child, somewhere along the way, I learned that it was safer to take up as little space as possible. Grief takes everything. I'm looking at words in order to see how those words reside in the world.

'

What carries me. A carriage. A memoir. A mother. A body, a book. My mother's birthday was six days ago. Outside, I find eggshells everywhere I walk. Blue starling's. White goldfinch's. Last year on her birthday, I found a cast-off robin's nest. I brought it home and put it on top of her plastic urn. I put flower petals in the bowl of it. But I couldn't say anything. This year, I took her name to the beach. I wrote it on a slip of paper. Renee made a tent with her body so I could light the yellow beeswax candles and then I gave my mother's name to the surf. One year, I'll make her a cake and throw it into the backyard like she used to do for me, all those years we weren't speaking. Right now, it's 10:38 p.m. I'm on my way to Manhattan. Mother's Day is this weekend. What takes me. From one place to another. What carries. What overwhelms. Takes me across. Or removes me entirely. To move, I get inside the belly of a thing.

'

The child in my mother. The mother in me, a mirror in my bones, my movements.

'

Life, be here. In the mornings. When the light is bone-colored and long. If she were, what would she. I have found something I did not expect.

All that time unravels, it builds. The earth and the people on its surface. In one sitting, hold me up to the light. What is trying to push through the membrane. The moments of clarity and of dispersal exist side by side. The turning of Earth and all that dissolves with each rotation. To stop here. Or here and here. Before ash and after bone. And the body. After itself.

*

I repair the past in the future of this fragment. A set of fractal patterns stored and restructured along the helical strands of my sentences. To bring light directly into the body. To reorder light through light. Recommunicating the cells.

*

To be the light that interrupts you.

To be weightless in the body of another.

Held and refracted. A splinter of bone. An eye. A petal. A cloud burst through the reading.

*

That we might feel this. Of existing at all. Filament to filament. Wherever our thoughts. Our desires. The moments that matter are all of them. To strike small matches. I meant to live.

,

To be reunited with the lost or forgotten. Language creates bonds of union between us. Reading turns our eyes inward. To see past the skin. Language tuned to visualize the invisible. To weave frequencies of light through the energy of thought: the light impulse transferred here. I want the interior of you to vibrate with my speaking. My lines, traveling the sensory thread of language, pendulate.

,

A psychic luminary: to articulate the unconscious encounter. All events in language move us toward the ephemeral and embodied at once. We are illumined, boundaryless. In proximity, we blur, a glossed zone, all accessed.

The phenomenon generated by language. What we're able to access through this temporary zone. What knowledge, what vibrational field.

,

When I was, I grieved for her. I grieved for her grief.

You are in the very hull of me.

'

Everything in running light, never motionless, parting the moments for us. So that we can get there. It's as if we are expected. In the world. Of it. Beside another. We realize it as we are on our way. Until we flurry up and do not appear again. I say, I am with others. I say, I am here. A bird, a birch tree. I am on and of the earth, but I am also carried off. Dispersed in the angles. A collection of transverse beams. Prisms and cracks, a parsing illuminated. I recognize it.

'

When my mother was alive she kept journals all over the house. She filled them with words and their etymologies, phone numbers, recipes, letters to no one, often all on the same page. She wrote, *cantilever*, *skein*. She wrote, *To find a good lawyer*. She wrote, *Monday, Memorial Day, 2006*. She wrote, *swarmiest*. She wrote, *You better be careful, or I'll take all of this away from you in a heartbeat*. She wrote, *All of this— I can take it away.* She wrote, *I just have to find someone.* Why didn't

my mother find someone. Why do women stay? *You better be careful
'cause I can make all this (our house) disappear for you. You better be
careful because I can take all this and make it disappear for you.*

'

Ululate. Ominous. Omen. Oleander. Mellifluous.

*She moved as silently as a fog. A rolling drum. So what you get addicted
to is not getting drunk. You get addicted to feeling better.*

Tacit. Ameliorate. Serpentine. Symbiosis. Nucleic.

The gift of a red bird.

Dilettante.

I'm getting fossilized in this house.

Travesty. God, what a travesty.

*To ruminate.
Rumination.*

Ruminative.

Ruminatively.

Ruminator.

I will manage to ruminate anyway.

The rest of the book is blank.

'

A thumbprint like an initiation, gathering energy at the corner of a
page. Her journals, after the wake of her.

'

I don't want to direct my gaze. A little way out. The land. The water.
Even the bottom of breathing. Broad beams of light, leaf-shaped. A fan-
ning into thin lines. A tracery. All which had appeared, but not clearly,
not formed. Appeared, but always out again in shadow.

'

I light a small word at the margin of the page to begin. Unfixed, uncen-terable, an over-exposure of the senses. To write with the intent of not-knowing, not needing to know, but only needing to reach that amorphous space, knowing it has everything I'd like to hold, be held by.

,

I don't want anything touching me, not even words.

I don't want anyone touching me, not even their words.

,

And between the two phrases, a cube is drawn in pencil. Below both phrases, a date, a time, and a room number, diagonally, margined off with an L-shaped line.

,

In other books, there are no dates only months marked. *10/*, it reads. 10/. She quotes the books she's reading. She writes about living for one's children. How to stand for something wonderful. She writes about what it means to hold anger. About silence, unbroken. She pens a TV movie's name below, *know it won't be broken.*

,

I didn't know my mother for the last seven years of her life. These books and their fragments are all I have of those years. And my memory of what the house had become. How we found it after her death, decaying.

,

I think I'm so busy with my thoughts, my mind is like a train pulling too many cars.

,

I have her handwriting like a network of fiber-optic cables to her cadence on some dayless day.

,

*The most important
things*

,

What is a woman? Some skin or story to put on. A body, poised, ready for every occasion. Hysteria and grace. Elegance and trash. A pendulum swinging in the gaze, the hips, the heritage. When I came to understand that I loved women. That I wanted to make a life as a woman alongside another woman, I felt the greatest sense of relief. I knew no lesbians. And this took all the stories out of me.

'

Form and the senses obliterated. My mother and I will never again stand in the same relation. And this has lifted something, erased something, proliferated other things. Getting to the other side of my grief is impossible, but within this space is like standing in an echo chamber, some hallway of ghosts passing like soft frequencies, palpable, forgiving.

'

A ghost, the noise we pass between us. And noise travels equally in all directions. Spherically through time. I wonder about dissipation and absorption. The re-rippling of noise through other noises. Your body next to mine next to a limitless number of ghosts. We are all beside our own speaking. I am the center of my own sphere but we all halo out.

'

In another life, I would have stayed to help her become the person she wanted to be but couldn't because of who knows what. Bipolarity, depression, drugs, alcohol, what it means to be a woman with a certain story to walk through, all the undiagnosed, unloved things. I would have stayed, but had I, who would I be. My mother is dead and I think she forgave me before she died. I've taken off my glasses. I can't see a thing. This is how I prepared for this book. Trying to get back to the sight in me where I first learned language. This edgeless place, where sight seems aquatic, haloed, amniotic. All borders obscured. A woman. A mother. A house. An ocean. Light. My voice, which sometimes sounds like hers.

,

My mother writes that she wants to become more like water.

Picture yourself as having the same qualities as water.

To have no inclination to be solid and hard. How all relation changes. A skein of water. A skein of light. Of all that's good and deserving of love.

,

The quarter-million-mile light of the moon. She was reading. She had filled the house with palm-sized stones. The weight of a hand in hers. We had all gone. We had to. She threatened us with murder if we stayed, and yet, I should have stayed.

'

Language like a light, like a sound, shuttered, shivered off. To enter into that lineage of light and alter something. I write to vibrate. To hold the various griefs and ruptures. Light to erase the borders between us. I build an acoustic architecture. You don't even have to move your body to travel through time. The horizon starts right beneath your thinking.

'

My mother made a list of twenty-one wishes in a journal. Number thirteen is: *To never be lonely again.*

'

At the periphery of language, in light, that space of blur between us. Nothing is ever stabilized. We are a series of intimate and divergent relations. But not to dissolve all categories, only to let them lean, conductive, porous, touched and touching at all times.

We should never be lonely.

,

I wake in the night and my body is resting just as yours does. I reach to a high shelf to put something away and the bones in my wrist are the bones in yours. I say something and you are in the room.

,

It's been a long time since we've talked. In this absence, I've done a lot of things. Right now, I'm living.

Mom, I've been reading this book about disaster. It's about how all things collapse, but also how they don't collapse. This book speaks of disaster as a wordless and silent space, as something that is impossible to talk about directly. I've come to understand that the most beautiful and possible things can happen in a collapsed place. Especially in writing and maybe even more especially in the body. Sometimes a disaster can make the body a more possible place to live within. I think this is because disasters can dislocate the self and suddenly it's possible to realize (or remember) you want your own form.

I live in a beautiful small home cluttered with magical things, houseplants, and books. And every day I have conversations with you like this. I tell you what I've been doing, all the things I love and that make me happiest. Like suddenly hearing the wind chimes sound or how I've started to make pizza dough by hand with Grandpa's recipe.

'

Later, quite some time later, you begin talking as if you have just woken up from a very, very long sleep. You are rejuvenated and healthy, as if you've just been born. You are so calm, trusting. I give you three glass jars: one of water, one of semolina, and one of a bright, warm light.

'

When you were a baby in your mother, I was a seed within you, an egg within your cells, listening to the sound of my grandmother's heartbeat.

'

I write a poem on the wall in pencil. The sun draws traceries of breathing light, then shadow, the trees. I take my hand and make a hollow over your name. I tumble your name in the bowl of my voice.

'

You are seven years old. Standing on the stoop of a brownstone in Brooklyn. You hold a small clamshell purse, not looking at the person behind the camera, your knees are exposed. Your hair is longer than I've ever seen it and I can tell you've been told to stand still.

,

In my body, I am seven years old in my bedroom. The window dressed in floor-to-ceiling nearly transparent curtains. It is morning and the window is wide, fully open to the sun and early spring day. The wind is wild. I can smell the bay and earth softening. Gull language, geese. The curtains undulate, billow, almost heave. I stand in the space created by the wind—between the window and the curtain, my back against the sill—and I watch the light convulse. My room, through the rippling skin of the curtain, blinking in and out of presence and tactility. The curtain licking my skin, flooding light, then shadow.

,

I've read that inherited traumas leave clues in our patterns of living and in the language we attempt to use to describe our emotional states. From where did I inherit this numbness. This body sometimes unrecognizable. An empathetic system that is often destabilizing. A body that disappears, leaving only the voice, unanchored. From where did I inherit this guilt, a survivor's guilt. For as long as I can remember, I have thought this was not my living that I was within. It belonged to someone else. Awake inside of me are disturbances that couldn't be resolved in one lifetime. My mother's silence killed her.

'

Imagine adjacent squares or houses, arms of an alphabet or body. Infuse their walls with light and they become blown out, bendable, suddenly pluralized into both themselves and something else. I flood the sentence with light until it breathes without me. I suspend a sound between two points. I strain the body into parts. Let it warp through the word.

'

Let this book be a haven for grieving. I read a book that asks me to tape a photo of you to the wall above my sleeping head. That I allow myself to fall asleep as if held. I am supposed to let myself sleep wrapped in your motherly love, accept it, blocking nothing. I'd rather this book hold me. No, that's a lie. When you would hold me, it could never last too long, as if you'd hit a threshold of feeling and have to shake me off. I was getting too close. I was comforted too much. Something in you was being met by me. And you'd poke it by poking me to unsettle whatever had opened in the space between our bodies. You told me once, that your mother did this to you also.

,

I've learned that traumas can be inherited, pass through the blood and hem themselves into the DNA. That they can sleep in your cells until the age they were experienced by your ancestors.

Something happened to me that never happened to me when I turned seven years old. To whom did it happen?

,

What is time when the body can hold the experience of another's living? In what time does healing occur?

,

I'm in my grandparent's basement. My childhood self is hiding and doesn't want to be found. I go upstairs, no one seems to be home, so I walk through all the rooms. I sit down at the desk to write myself a letter to find later. In the kitchen, the green rotary phone. I want to call my aunt, but I'm not sure what time I'm in. My grandparents, my mother, and I come in from shopping. They unpack their bags as if I'm not there. They're cutting up a loaf of semolina, salting the warm mozzarella. My grandfather is about to make sauce from the garden's plum tomatoes. I'm watching them eat. I'd like to stay. My childhood self is eating chunks of pecorino. Broccoli rabe. I can't hear what they're saying. They don't see me.

I look around the backyard at all the places I love. The gnarled knuckles of the crab apple trees. The statue of Mary in the crescent of cedars I like to talk to. The place where only moss will grow. The ugly dog next door.

I ask my mother if she'd like to go for a drive. There's a loop—we're backing out of the driveway—it's taking a long time to happen. I'm nervous because I don't want to fight with her. The scene is stuck, she is not really there. I grab her by the arms. I'm shaking her. Yelling. Why isn't she seeing me. I feel overwhelmed yelling her name, Mom, over and over again. She pales, disappears and I'm left throwing a tantrum by myself.

/

Transfixed together. Rooted in a delicate, invisible repatterning of light.

/

I talk to you every day by the bay where we used to steal pumpkins.

I will see you very soon!

ı

I let my voice fall apart so that I can access the ephemeral. All things beyond speech, beneath and within all sounds and irreducible distances. That halo at the threshold, given off, occupied by what can only be described as a blur of silence so near to sound that the memory of sound disorients all things. I draw as near as I'm able. When I learned that linearity has never been reliable, when I was interrupted, when I remembered, this uncertainty united all things.

ı

Thank you for listening
Thank you for your kindness
Thank you for your love
And concern without judgement

I will see you very soon!

ı

I'm in the garden now, collecting seeds. Tomato. Eggplant. Peppers. Peas. The house begins to shudder. A tarp on the roof, the concrete deck my grandfather built in rubble, the windows are dirty. My younger self can't see me, but she's alone sitting on the lawn, so I go sit beside her. No one's home, so I can't leave her. She's only three. I will take her with me. There's my car seat, already in the car. We're in the driveway loop; I'm putting her in the car seat for a very long time. I think how lovely she is and how much I love her.

'

To gain access to those no longer of the body, I need only retreat further into my own. To access that blur, that glossed space at the edge of sight, almost-seeing, almost-articulation, almost-memory. The undercurrent as it travels, as it vibrates, as electricity jumps the gap. That moment elongated and looked upon with a sight that comes from some elsewhere other than the eyes.

'

I have her papers, but she is not in them, only her thinking as it unraveled, as she attempted to stitch herself into time. Her grief is there, her irregularities and paranoias, her loneliness, her rage. I might not even be here for her, not even for the memory of her, but for whatever is hemmed into my cells that can still touch her in some other time. That can still touch the women before the woman that was my mother.

'

If I could offer you a book that hums, that unsharpens your being, that undulates, that opens a refuge for whatever is behind thinking when thinking rests, expands, incubating movement and growth, gathering energy at the regions between what is solid and what isn't.

'

I don't know what was hidden in my mother's body and her mother's body before her. I come from a family of secrets, everything "kept in the family," rerouted into silence. I'll never know what I've inherited, but I've given myself the task of working it out, through language, through the act of looking into what I can't see, but only feel at the edge of myself.

'

At the level of my cells: an eternal geometric structure that binds, harmonizes, shapes, and transforms the whole body, at all scales, from the subatomic to astronomical. Light's dilation. Repairing. This intelligent quantum field.

'

I pick up light. I pick it up with both hands, shake the rope of it into a page. I put it in my mouth. I let it pull a sound through me. The desire to lean against a thing through language as light might lean across my house. Its dissipating gloss across the bedroom, spilling the kitchen. I'm alone, so I lay my body in its way. I put it on like a wound. Watch my finger's translucence. I think about the membrane of the page, illu-mined in its reading. But this isn't right. So, I make sounds into the room until the light is pulled from my house back into the city.

'

Take it as a gift of light. *I forgive you.*

'

Through light. Through language. Cells and genealogy. The carriage of one's body. And what comes after—

'

I draw a circle around us in a forest. Meridian of sound, pathway, tide—I'm trying to make lights move through your body. I'm in the ocean now, swimming toward a boat. It is my father's. He pulls me from the water. I'm my childhood self. He puts a lifejacket on me and tucks me into the boat. I want to ask my father if I'm okay, but he doesn't have a face, just a revolving door. I'm climbing in my childhood bedroom window now. It's dusk and I can hear you make dinner in the kitchen. I go to set the table. I want to ask you if you can be happy like this, here, forever. I can't see your face. I just keep setting the table. Everything keeps happening, as if we're all shuffling cards.

,

I'm even younger now. I pull you out into the backyard. We water marigolds, fuchsias, Johnny-jump-ups. To stay in the dusk-near-dark watering flowers. I tell you you don't have to die, but you can't hear me. We're not there. I take your hand in mine. My hand is a wing, a cocoon, a comfort. You don't have to. I turn you into a hummingbird, cradling you gently.

,

Pinhole and tube into the earth. The wet channel of my own voice, emptying. Absorb. Transmute. Now what did happen is one of a million.

,

I am three weeks old. I bring the healing forward.

,

My mother. Where she grew and was protected. Pattern stages. First, the shoots, then the magnificent bending of bones. Alternate. Deep green. Then the hidden, before the turn. I recall the pattern. It was growth.

,

The thick rope of her DNA with my own. To continue. This is when I began.

,

Matter and energy, resolving. In the beginning, everything. To have occupied a single infinitely dense point. A complex singularity of self. To reach that point of singularity before explosion. The curvature of forever until we begin to move in reverse.

,

Language allows for connective resonance. I come to language because I want to heal something inside of me. Something hemmed into the cells,

passed across generations, between mouths and mothers. To reattune
myself through articulated frequencies. I yield to the hidden voice.
Of bone and light at once. Having access to the unlit through what is
illuminated.

'

I set my mother's notebooks out in the sun. Pass her sentences
through a cellular light. To heal the past in the future of this thought.
The face of my grandmother. My great grandmother's hands, resting.
I make myself fragile for you. Because we hold vigil for one another in
language. Because we need to ingest light and release it.

'

My cells, a current of folds, water, light. To not be afraid to be seen.
A crosscurrent: the aura emitted through the weave of cellular matter.
Glowing and reconfigured. Of energy, of light, a weather system within.
Moving memory, shame, all I've inherited. Unknow the trauma stored in
the clavicle. The pain in the tailbone. The numbness in the womb.

'

Nearly a decade has passed, and I only now feel the mending of the field. No longer filament or cilia, but sphere. A messenger underwater. Diaphanous light-being, the ocean of my body. I pass light through the water—words in water, striated in salt, to repattern the code.

*

How life can only have arisen from life. I am breathing the light of a star, the ocean in my grandmother. This biological fulcrum. DNA coiled, bundled and condensed, released. The helix, the vessel of me, the muscles a mirror of water as it moves, vessel to vessel, holding it all together. A vortex ring, and then another, rising up through the water of my voice.

Light

'

When we are not yet born, we are also ten. We feel our birth a thousand
miles away. We see a body suspended across the sky. We come cleaved
at birth. We are both zero and eleven. We are an irregularity draped
across a country. We are here, we say. We are here. We are uncusped
at the threshold. Tangential at the curve. A compendium of skins. A skin-
ning sound. We are flooded. We are emanated. We are a mesh of strings,
striated, invisible. We are a single canopy. A permeable membrane,
molecular, wet at the lips.

'

When we are not yet born, we feel our birth a thousand
miles away. We see a body suspended across the sky. We come cleaved
at birth. We are both zero and eleven. We are an irregularly draped
across a country. We are here, we say. We are here. We are uncusped
at the threshold. Tangential at the curve. A compendium of skins, a skin-
ning sound. We are flooded. We are emanated. We are a mesh of strings,
striated, invisible. We are a single canopy. A permeable membrane,
molecular, wet at the lips.

'

When we are thirty-four, we are cartographers of empty space. We map
a fertile grid. We map the shifting grid between. Between thought and
body. Between bodies. We reverberate. We scatter but keep relation. We
specter we. We are a dream-culture of intimacies. We write ourselves
to return to ourselves. When we are forty-one, we split our house in
two and then stitch it together. When we arrive at the other, we create
a burst of reference. A globe of hatch-marks knit skin to skin.

'

Our words are creatures across an open room.

Our words are creatures across an open room.

*

We are cosseted, a living alphabet along the ground. We let ourselves be turned. When we are, we are always writing. Even before the sentence begins, it has begun. It is a transmutation through the tongue. A membranous correspondence.

*

We are cosseted, a living alphabet along the ground. We let ourselves
be turned. When we are, we are always writing. Even before the sen-
tence begins, it has begun. It is a transmutation through the tongue.
A membranous correspondence.

'

When we are. When we are one, we are also twelve. When we are
twelve, we are as lonely as if we were one. When we are lonely, we let
our tongues reach out until they touch another's.

'

When we are. When we are one, we are also twelve. When we are
twelve, we are as lonely as if we were one. When we are lonely, we let
our tongues reach out until they touch another's.

'

We want you to reach for us. We are the alphabet realigned, unarchived against the body. We say, this is a book. A body. We say, this is a sentence. We say, my mouth is a living record. We say, a bright latticework, a netting. We say, watch. We watch this net breathe as it reconfigures itself between us. We say, this is a thing that makes shape and takes it. We say, this is not a border, or bed. We say, inlets. Sound.

POSTSCRIPT

Syntax: a bioluminescence

For over a decade, I have been mesmerized by the intelligence and adaptability of the biophoton field. That nonlinear, but highly structured and lucid netting of light woven between the cells of all living bodies. Those transmitters and receivers of energy across the electromagnetic spectrum. Carriers of information, narrative, experience, and the epigenetic regulation of gene expression and memory within all living systems, ordering all life processes. I've learned through study and through close engagement with my own field of cellular light as well as broader fields of earthen and astral light that the bioluminescence of our cells and our epigenetic memories are intelligent, cosmic in scale, and are endlessly adaptable. And just as they remember damaging (*and* beautiful) impressions, they are also able to be repaired, rerouted, re-sequenced.

In my work as a poet, I am devoted to the ways a book, as an extended ceremonial field of a body, might serve as a site of radical transformation. How the poem, the fragment, the lyric essay, and even the silences between sounds might serve as nonlinear conduits for transmuting a body and its consciousness. I think about the biological field and the dynamic relationship between a book and a body. I think about the body—holder of light and memory across generations—and how language, by way of the book, undulates within an always fluctuating and organic space created each time a book is opened and read. I position myself, as I write, within this fluctuation.

I see words as subtle energy carriers, direct conduits to the material and immaterial of a body. I see narrative practice as a modality for healing, as a way of moving energy, of recalibrating and quieting light. I attune the body at the level of the line. To *language* is to take part in transmission, transmutation of energy, sonic repatterning of biological light. To reorganize the grammars within. To find and heal a body, a lineage, that has, for much of my life, felt impossible, in distress, indistinct.

I have come to believe we can heal aspects of the past by pulling them through the fractal of the poem. The movement of words, the texture of a sound, the way information is conveyed through the sensory thread of language has a recuperative *and* retroactive effect on the body. That is to say: within language structures and their propensity to fragment is a nonlinear but organizing force that can reach into a body and transmute—through a careful patterning of sound and semantics—the body and its consciousness across times and generations.

If we understand the poem as a diagram of energetic connections, we can also say that it is a mode of energy work capable of rerouting the body's unseen energy fields. If we understand syntax as a direct conduit to the biological field, we can also say that innovations in syntax allow for innovations in consciousness, memory, and gene expression all working together to develop a more possible and healthier form.

This intention—initiating bodily and epigenetic healing through syntax—is what glows at the core of my triptych of poetic texts: *Between Grammars*, *The Way a Line Hallucinates Its Own Linearity*, and finally, *A Library of Light*. I have been rewritten by these books.

It took me over a decade to complete the ceremony that is *A Library of Light* and now you hold it in your hands. May you, dear reader, be taken up, held in your own ceremony of healing while reading. Thank you for being here with me.

Acknowledgments

Deepest gratitude

to the visionary work of Swiss telepathic healer, researcher, and artist Emma
Kunz, whose channeled drawings, which served for her as both research
and remedy, I held close and consulted over the many years of writing this
book.

to *Photo 51*, the earliest X-ray crystallography photograph demonstrating the
double-helix structure of DNA, which I kept in conversation with a small
archive of my mother's journals, family photographs, ancestral documents,
and the works of Emma Kunz.

to the Snæfellsnes Peninsula of Iceland, the Lofoten Islands of Norway, and
the waters of the Long Island Sound where I wrote and edited much of this
manuscript over the years.

to the flower essence of Bleeding Heart.

to the writings of biologist Nessa Carrey, biophysicist Fritz-Albert Popp, and
somatic psychologist Peter A Levine.

to all at Essay Press for publishing early excerpts of *A Library of Light* as an
e-chapbook titled *In Resonance: translations of light in language*.

to Nadia Hironaka and Maryland Institute College of Art, Norræna húsið in
Reykjavík, Iceland, Hollis Mickey and RISD Museum, and Amaranth Borsuk
and Jeanne Heuving at the University of Washington at Bothell for hosting

public ceremonies and memory altars for *A Library of Light*. And to all who trusted me with their memories of mothers, language, and light. I hold them dear.

to Samantha Shay, KÁRYYN, Nini Julia Bang, Victoria Sendra, and all luminaries of Source Material Collective for their visionary and alchemical work when transmuting *A Library of Light* into the experimental opera *of Light*. Samantha, our collaborations and conversations across this past decade about the transformative powers of theater, performance, and poetry have been so vital and nourishing. May we dream through one another's works for a very long time.

to angela rawlings, whose friendship and brilliance have been a buoying force since the earliest days of writing this book. Thank you for sharing Iceland with me and for hosting that salon in 2012 in your home in Reykjavík where I met Samantha Shay and read the earliest pages of this book while glowing in the light of the midnight summer sun.

to Jen Bervin, Shell Rose, Michael Braithwaite, Amra Brooks, John Cayley, Joanna Howard, Charlotte Lagarde, Sara Renee Marshall, Mathias Svalina, Suzanna Tamminen, Mike Vogel, Erin Ward, and Therese Workman for their friendship, their love of sharing food and laughter, and the endless conversations about the grieving body, ghosts, light, and writing. I love you all so much.

to Renee Gladman, my love, for being my forest. For holding the ground. For building the bower and corridor to writing through which I was able to begin writing this book.

About the Author

Danielle Vogel is a poet, lyric essayist, and interdisciplinary artist working at the intersections of queer ecology, somatics, and ceremony. She is the author of four hybrid poetry collections, including *Edges & Fray: on language, presence and (invisible) animal architectures* (Wesleyan University Press, 2020), and a triptych of poetic texts: *Between Grammars* (Noemi Press, 2015), *The Way a Line Hallucinates Its Own Linearity* (Red Hen Press, 2020), and *A Library of Light* (Wesleyan University Press, 2024). Her installations and site-responsive works have been displayed at RISD Museum, among other art venues, and adaptations of her work have been performed at such places as Carnegie Hall in New York and the Tjarnarbíó Theater in Reykjavík, Iceland. Vogel is an associate professor at Wesleyan University, where she teaches workshops in innovative poetics, memory and memoir, and composing across the arts. She makes her home in the Connecticut River Valley where she also runs a private practice as an herbalist and flower-essence practitioner.